*From the moment the first snowdrop appears, garden flowers all give great pleasure throughout the year. This book will help to identify those you do not know and tell you a little more about those you do.*

*Acknowledgments:*
The photograph on the front endpaper is by Tim Clark; those on pages 13 (top), 14, and 16 (bottom left and right) are by courtesy of the Natural History Photographic Agency.

First Edition

# Garden Flowers

*Written and photographed*
*by* Harry Stanton

Ladybird Books  Loughborough

## Snowdrops

The always-nodding white flower of the snowdrop is one of the first to appear each spring. It makes a fine cut flower and it will grow in almost any soil.

*Height 10 to 20 cm*          *Flower size 20 to 25 mm*
*Flowering January to March*   *Perennial bulb*

## Chionodoxa

Also known as Glory of the Snow, these flowers bloom as early as the snowdrops and make a fine display. A very good plant for rockeries.

*Height 15 cm*
*Flowering February*
*Flower size 1 to 2 cm*
*Perennial bulb*

### Forsythia

Almost the earliest flowering shrub to be seen, forsythia's yellow flowers appear before the leaves. The flowers grow on new twigs so it must be pruned soon after flowering.

*Height up to 4 or 5 metres*
*Flowering February to April*

*Flower size 2 to 3 cm*
*Perennial shrub*

### Crocuses

One of the first flowers to be seen each year, the crocus grows in ordinary garden soil but it needs sunshine for the flowers to open. The bulbs should be left to multiply for four or five years and then lifted and divided.

*Height 10 to 15 cm*
*Flowering February to May*
*Flower size 3 to 5 cm*
*Perennial*
*The autumn crocus flowers from*
*  September to October*

### Grape Hyacinths

Often found in rock gardens and in borders. They need a sunny place in ordinary soil. Bulbs should be planted 10 cm deep in autumn.

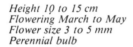

*Height 10 to 15 cm*
*Flowering March to May*
*Flower size 3 to 5 mm*
*Perennial bulb*

## Polyanthuses

A member of the primula family. It does not mind a shaded position, although it does not like dry soil. After flowering, the plants can be divided up to make more for the next year.

*Height 10 to 20 cm*
*Flowering March to May*
*Flower size 2 to 3 cm*
*Perennial*

## Daffodils

Daffodils can be grown in flower beds, lawns or in bowls indoors. They are excellent for cutting and last well in a vase of water. Daffodils grow well in any part of the garden, even in the shade.
When the flowers have finished, the leaves should not be removed until they have withered.

*Height 10 to 50 cm*
*Flowering April*
*Flower size 3 to 6 cm*
*Perennial*

7

## Narcissi

The narcissus is very similar to a daffodil, except that it has a shorter trumpet often with red, white or yellow in the flowers.

*Height 15 to 45 cm*
*Flowering April to May*
*Flower size 3 to 5 cm*
*Perennial bulb*

## Hyacinths

Hyacinths have a wonderful scent. The bulbs need a rich well-drained soil and they can be grown in bowls, tubs, window boxes and flower beds.

*Height 25 to 30 cm*
*Flowering April to May*
*Flower size 1 to 2 cm*
*Perennial bulb*

## *Aubretia*

Grown on rockeries or in flower beds this spreading plant may have violet, mauve, purple or white flowers. Seeds can be planted, but it is easier to divide older plants or plant offshoots.

*Height 10 to 15 cm*
*Flowering April to May*
*Flower size 1 to 2 cm*
*Perennial*

## Honesty

Not only is honesty a pretty spring flower with its white or purple petals, but it is also valued for its silvery paperlike seed heads which are used in dried flower displays.

*Height 30 cm to 1 metre*
*Flowering April to June*

*Flower size 10 to 18 mm*
*Biennial*

◀

## Rhododendrons

There are many varieties of this shrub, which can grow into a tall tree. Most of the plants are evergreen, but all of them have the most beautiful flowers. The plant does not like soil with lime in it, but otherwise it is easy to grow.

▶

*Height 1 to 12 metres*
*Flowering April to June*
*Flower size 1 to 3 cm*
*Perennial*

## Irises

The large flowers of the iris family are unlike any other garden flower. They need a sunny position. The roots, which look like long potatoes, should be planted half in and half out of the soil.

Yellow Flags are members of the iris family, but they only grow on the edges of ponds, streams, and in marshes.

*Height 50 cm to 1 metre*      *Flower size 3 to 12 cm*
*Flowering April to July*      *Perennial*

### Wallflowers

Used as a spring bedding plant together with tulips, wallflowers have a delicious scent and a wide range of colours. Seeds sown in summer should be transplanted to where they are to flower in autumn.

*Height 25 to 60 cm*
*Flowering April to July*
*Flower size 1 to 2 cm*
*Perennial, grown as biennial*

### Tulips

The single blooms of the tulip are one of the best cut flowers. They like a rich well-drained soil. There are many varieties, and all are easy to grow.

*Height 15 cm to 1 metre*
*Flowering April to July*
*Flower size 3 to 7 cm*
*Perennial bulb*

## Calendulas

These are also called Common or Pot Marigolds, because the flowers can be used to flavour soups.
It is an easy plant to grow, and because it seeds so freely it may become a weed. It can be grown with both single and double flowers, in even the poorest soil.

*Height 30 to 60 cm*
*Flowering April to October*
*Flower size 3 to 7 cm*
*Hardy annual*

### *Aquilegia*

These flowers can be orange, violet, yellow or white. They like a rich soil which is not too moist, although they must be well watered in dry weather. They make a fine cut flower and can be grown from seeds planted in spring, or by dividing older plants in autumn.

*Height 30 to 65 cm*
*Flowering May to June*
*Flower size 3 to 4 cm*
*Perennial*

## Magnolias

In spring magnolias are the most beautiful of all trees and shrubs, with their large lily-like flowers. They need a good soil and enjoy a sheltered position.

*Height 1 to 15 metres*
*Flowering May to June*
*Flower size 5 to 20 cm*
*Perennial*

## Lilies of the Valley

A dainty flower with a strong scent. It likes cool moist soil with some shade. The flowers look their best if planted in large groups.

*Height 15 to 30 cm*
*Flowering May to June*
*Flower size 5 to 10 mm*
*Perennial*

## Solomon's Seal

A useful perennial plant for a shady part of the garden.
This flower, once planted, should not be disturbed.

*Height 60 to 90 cm*          *Flower size 2 to 20 mm*
*Flowering May to June*

## Campanulas

The word campanula means *little bell* and this describes
the shape of the flowers of this large family of plants.
The flowers, which need a sunny position, can be blue,
violet, white or pink.

*Height 70 cm to 1 metre*
*Flowering May to August*
*Flower size 3 to 4 cm*
*Biennial*

## *Mesembryanthemums*

This plant is also known as the Livingstone Daisy. The flowers will only open in the sunshine, but the plant will grow in poor soil.

*Height 3 to 6 cm*
*Flowering May to August*
*Flower size 2 to 6 cm*

*Both annual and perennial*
*   species*

## *Ox-eye Daisies*

Ox-eye daisies will grow in most soils. They do not mind some shade. They need little attention except that they should be cut back after flowering.

*Height 30 to 50 cm*
*Flowering May to August*
*Flower size 3 to 5 cm*
*Perennial*

### *Foxgloves*

A plant which can grow in the semi-shade, the foxglove can be found in many gardens. It can have rosy-purple, cream, white or pink flowers. Once grown, the plant seeds itself for the following year.

*Height 60 cm to 1.5 metres*
*Flowering May to September*
*Flower size 2 to 3 cm*
*Biennial*

### *Cornflowers*

Cornflowers will grow almost anywhere. They are grown as a cut flower. Seeds planted in early spring will flower in May and the seedlings should not be moved as they do not transplant well. The most common colour is blue, but pink, white and violet flowers are grown.

*Height 30 cm to 1 metre*
*Flowering May to October*
*Flower size 3 to 6 cm*
*Annual*

18

## *Poppies*

Poppies found in our gardens came from many parts of the world. The blooms often only last for a day or two, but they have many bright flowers which can make a fine showing.

19

### California Poppies

A plant which is easily grown from seeds sown out-of-doors in April. The flowers need a sunny position, although they will grow in the poorest and driest of soils.

*Height 30 to 70 cm*
*Flowering May to October*
*Flower size 3 to 6 cm*
*Annual*

## June onwards

### Peonies

Although they flower for only a short time, the large flowers of the peony come at a time when spring flowers are dying and before summer flowers are appearing. These plants should not be transplanted, as they may not flower for another three years if moved.

*Height 60 cm to 1 metre*          *Flower size 10 to 25 cm*
*Flowering June*                     *Perennial*

### *Azaleas*

Azaleas are members of the rhododendron family. They begin as a small shrub, and can grow into large tree-like bushes.

*Height up to 6 metres*
*Flowering June to July*
*Flower size 2 to 4 cm*
*Perennial*

### *Delphiniums*

The flowers of the delphinium are usually various shades of blue, violet and mauve, but some varieties are white, yellow and red. If the flower spikes are cut off after flowering, more blooms will appear later in the year.

*Height 30 cm to 1.3 metres*
*Flowering June to July*
*Flower size 5 to 20 cm*
*Perennial*

## *Lupins*

Lupins will grow in almost any well-drained soil if it does not have too much lime. If cut back after flowering, the plant will produce flowers again later in the year.

*Height 1 to 1.5 metres*
*Flowering June to July*

*Flower size 1 to 2 cm*
*Perennial*

## *Pinks*

Suitable for flower beds and for cutting, this plant has been a favourite of gardeners for centuries, as it has a delightful scent.

*Height 15 to 30 cm*
*Flowering June to July*
*Flower size 2 to 4 cm*
*Perennial*

## Virginia Stock

Virginia stock will grow in any soil and it is extremely useful for border edgings. Although it may be sown in spring it flowers better when sown in autumn.

*Height 6 to 10 cm*
*Flowering June and July*
*Flower size 10 mm*
*Hardy annual*

## Mullein

Mullein often have interesting woolly leaves. Most mullein plants have yellow flowers, but some varieties have reddish purple blooms.

*Height 60 cm to 2.3 metres*
*Flowering June to July*
*Flower size 2 to 3 cm*
*Perennial or biennial*

23

## Clematis

Clematis are beautiful plants. There are many varieties. Most are climbers which support themselves with leaf stalks which curl round twigs, trellis and branches. They need a sunny position and a rich soil.

*Height 30 cm to 10 metres*
*Flowering June to August*
*Flower size 2 to 15 cm*
*Perennial*

◀
## Echium

These flowers grow profusely with heads of rose, lavender or blue flowers. Seeds should be sown in spring in a sunny position where the plants are to flower.

▶

*Height 90 cm to 1 metre*
*Flowering June to August*
*Flower size 5 to 10 cm*
*Hardy annual*

## *Gypsophila*

Sometimes known as the chalk plant because of its clouds of small white flowers. It will grow in most soils and it does not mind half-shade.

*Height 75 cm to 1.2 metres*
*Flowering June to August*
*Flower size 1 to 2 mm*
*Perennial*

### Salvia

A member of the sage family, this is a splendid summer bedding plant which needs a sunny position in a good soil. After sowing under glass in spring, the plants should not be put out until the risk of frost has passed.

*Height 30 to 45 cm*
*Flowering June to August*
*Flower size, spikes of flowers,*
  *15 cm long*
*Half-hardy annual*

### Sweet Williams

Although it is really a perennial, sweet william is usually grown as a biennial. Seed sown in May should be transplanted to the flowering position in autumn. It is a good flower for cutting and has a strong scent and a wide range of colours.

*Height 30 to 60 cm*           *Flower size 2 to 4 cm*
*Flowering June to August*     *Perennial, grown as biennial*

## China Asters

These are good flowers for cutting, because they last a long time in water. They like to grow in a sunny place. They can be sown where they are to flower, or planted out when the frosts are over.

*Height 30 to 75 cm*
*Flowering June to September*
*Flower size 9 to 15 cm*
*Annual*

## Clarkia

Clarkia grows best in a well-drained soil and in sunshine. Care has to be taken with the plants as they tend to snap off at soil level. If cut, the flowers only keep if all the leaves are stripped off.

*Height 45 to 60 cm*
*Flowering June to September*
*Flower size 3 to 5 cm*
*Annual*

### Geums

Geums will grow in almost any soil. They are very popular in the garden because they stay in flower for a long time. Although perennials, they are grown as biennials. Seeds are sown in the summer, and the plants transplanted to where they are to flower the following May.

*Height 30 to 60 cm*
*Flowering June to September*
*Perennial, grown as biennial*

### Larkspurs

Another plant which likes a light soil and full sunshine. The flower is excellent for cutting, and many different colours are to be seen. Seeds should be sown where they are to flower, as they do not like to be transplanted.

*Height 60 cm to 1 metre*
*Flowering June to September*
*Flower size 1 to 3 cm*
*Annual*

## *Lavender*

A grey shrub whose flowers have a beautiful scent.
There are varieties with both blue and white flowers. It
will grow in most soils provided it is warm. New plants
can be raised by taking cuttings during late spring and
early summer.
Dried lavender flowers in small bags are often used to
perfume linen.

*Height 30 to 90 cm*
*Flowering June to September*

*Flower size 2 to 3 mm*
*Perennial shrub*

## *Love-in-a-mist*

A plant which should be
sown where it is to flower.
Even after it has flowered
the leaves remain
attractive.

*Height 30 to 50 cm*
*Flowering June to September*
*Flower size 2 to 4 cm*
*Annual*

## *Phlox*

Phlox have some of the most brilliantly coloured flowers to be seen in the garden. They need a rich well-drained soil in a sunny position. The roots should be divided every three years to prevent the flowers becoming smaller.

*Height 15 cm to 1.5 metres*
*Flowering June to September*
*Flower size 1 to 5 cm*
*Perennial*

## *Sweet Peas*

Good soil is necessary to grow sweet peas. They make excellent cut flowers. The plants are trained to grow up canes or a trellis and, if fed properly, up to five or six blooms may grow on each stalk.

*Height 1 to 3 metres*
*Flowering June to September*
*Flower size 2 to 4 cm*
*Annuals*

### *Tagetes*

These half-hardy annuals
are members of the
marigold family.
The small yellowish
flowers clustered closely
together make good
bedding plants.

*Height 30 to 45 cm*
*Flowering June to September*
*Flower size 1 to 2 cm*
*Half-hardy annual*

### *African Marigolds*

A free-growing and
attractive flower which
looks its best when plants
are placed close together.
It is not a good plant for
cutting, as its leaves and
stem smell unpleasant.

*Height 30 cm to 1.5 metres*
*Flowering June to October*
*Flower size 5 to 20 cm*
*Annual*

31

### *Antirrhinums*

Known as snapdragons, antirrhinums will grow in almost any kind of soil, especially if they are in a sunny position. Seed should be sown under glass in March and the young plants set out in the flower beds in May.

*Height 45 to 90 cm*
*Flowering June to October*
*Flower size 2 to 5 cm*
*Annual*

### *Annual Chrysanthemums*

These are excellent flowers for cutting and they have a wide range of colours. They are easy to grow, and the seeds should be sown in April where they are to flower.

*Height 45 to 90 cm*
*Flowering June to October*
*Flower size 5 to 7 cm*

32

## *Begonias*

There are two main varieties of begonia. The tuberous begonia has large double flowers with a wide range of colours.
The fibrous-rooted begonia has small flowers.
Both types have to be raised in a warm greenhouse as they cannot tolerate the cold.

*Height 30 to 45 cm*
*Flowering June to October*

*Flower size:*
*Tuberous 10 to 15 cm*
*Fibrous 2 to 4 cm*
*Half-hardy perennial*

## Candytufts

There are both perennial and annual varieties of candytuft. All of them have dense flower heads with white or lilac flowers. It is a good plant for rockeries and flower beds.

*Height 15 to 45 cm*
*Flowering:*
  *Annuals June to October*
  *Perennials April to June*
*Flower size 2 to 4 mm*

◄
## Fuchsia

A graceful shrub, covered in unusual bright red flowers, which grows especially well near the seaside. New plants can be grown from cuttings taken in the spring.

►

*Height 1 to 2 metres*
*Flowering June to October*
*Flower size 2 to 5 cm*
*Perennial shrub*

## *Chinese Lanterns*

This is a plant which will grow in almost any soil and because it has spreading roots it can become a nuisance. The flowers are attractive and the seed pods form lanterns for dried flower decorations.

*Height 30 to 90 cm*
*Flowering June to October*
*Flower size 18 to 25 mm*
*Lantern 2 to 5 cm*
*Perennial*

### Helichrysums
### *(Everlasting Flower)*

A member of the daisy
family whose flowers will
keep their shape and
colour throughout the
winter if they are gathered
early and allowed to dry
with their heads hung
downwards.

Seeds can be sown under
glass in February or where
they are to flower when
the frosts have finished.

*Height 60 to 90 cm*
*Flowering June to October*
*Flower size 3 to 5 cm*
*Annual*

### Geraniums

Although this popular
flower is commonly called
a geranium, it is not a
geranium at all. It is really
a pelargonium. Plants can
only be put in the flower
beds after the frosts have
finished. Ordinary soil is
good enough, but the
flowers need full sunlight.

*Height 30 to 60 cm*
*Flowering June to October*
*Flower size 1 to 3 cm*
*Perennial*

## Lobelias

Lobelia is used as an edging plant. It is also planted in window boxes and hanging baskets as it blooms for most of the summer. Seeds should be sown under glass in March, and the plants transplanted to where they are to flower in May.

*Height 10 to 15 cm*
*Flowering June to October*
*Flower size 5 to 8 mm*
*Annual*

## Gladioli

A beautiful flower often grown for cutting. The corms should be planted 5 to 10 cm deep in a damp sunny place in April. The flowers need stakes to hold them up. In autumn the corms should be dug up, dried and stored away from frost for the next year.

*Height 40 cm to 1.9 metres*
*Flowering June to October*
*Flower size 2 to 5 cm*
*Perennial*

## Roses

Roses have been the favourite flower of gardeners for many centuries. Different varieties have been bred, using plants from all over the world.

Both hybrid tea and floribunda roses may be grown on different kinds of root stock as standard or climbing plants.

With all roses, dead flowerheads should be picked off to encourage more blossoms later in the season.

Roses should be cut back in winter, but before doing so, get advice from an experienced gardener.

### Hybrid Tea Roses

Hybrid tea are the roses with large flowers which grow singly.

*Height 60 cm to 1.2 metres*
*Flowering June to October*
*Flower size 5 to 20 cm*

## Rambling or Climbing Roses

These roses can be trained to grow up a wall, trellis, or post.

*Height 1 to 4 metres*
*Flowering June to October*

## Floribunda Roses

Floribundas are roses with flowers which grow in bunches or clusters.

*Height 60 cm to 1.2 metres*
*Flowering June to October*
*Flower size 4 to 8 cm*

## Standard Roses

These roses have a tall rootstock. They look like small trees with flowers at the top.

*Height 1.5 to 2 metres*
*Flowering June to October*

## *Pansies*

Pansies will grow in most soils if they are in a sunny place. In a rich soil, they do not mind a little shade. Seed sown in the summer will produce plants which should be planted out in autumn to flower the following summer.

*Height 15 to 25 cm*
*Flowering June to October*
*Flower size 2 to 3 cm*
*Biennial*

## *Sweet Alyssum*

Sweet Alyssum is used as an edging plant around flower beds. It is easily grown, and the seeds should be sown in spring where they are to flower. White, violet, pink and purple flowers can be grown.

*Height 15 cm*
*Flowering June to October*
*Flower size 5 mm*
*Annual*

### Ten Week Stock

A flower with a beautiful scent. As it lasts when cut, it is a favourite with gardeners. Seeds should be sown the previous summer or early in spring.

*Height 30 to 75 cm*
*Flowering June to October*

*Flower size 1 to 2 cm*
*Annual or biennial*

## *July onwards*

### Carnations

Carnations have a most attractive scent and are very suitable for cutting. They grow well in flower beds. Good single blooms are best grown under glass — all the side buds are removed, leaving just one to develop.
Colours vary from white and yellow, to pink and red.

*Height 30 to 40 cm*
*Flowering July to August*
*Flower size 3 to 5 cm*
*Perennial*

## Hollyhocks

One of the tallest plants to be seen in the garden, so they need staking or planting against a wall to save them from the effect of strong winds. The flowers can be almost any colour. They will survive for many years, but they are often grown as biennials.

*Height 1.5 to 3 metres*
*Flowering July to September*
*Flower size 5 to 10 cm*
*Perennial*

## Lilies

There are many kinds of lily. All of them need a well-drained soil. Often they are planted among other flowers, to keep their roots in the shade. Once planted, they should not be disturbed unless it is unavoidable.

**Regal Lily ▶**

**Day Lily** The flowers only last for one day, but the plant flowers from mid-spring until late summer.
**Bourbon Lily** The national flower of France, which has a delightful scent. It can grow to a height of two metres.
◀ **Tiger Lily** The bulbs of this beautiful flower are grown as food in Japan and China.

*Flowering July to September*

## Mallows

An easily-grown plant which flowers throughout the summer. Sow in its flowering position in March and thin out as it does not like being transplanted.

*Height 60 cm to 1.2 metres*
*Flowering July to September*
*Flower size 4 to 10 cm*
*Annual*

## *Petunias*

If well watered and in a sunny position, petunias have a mass of brilliant flowers. Dead flowers should be removed to stop seed pods developing, and to encourage more flowers to bloom.

*Height 20 to 80 cm*  *Flower size 4 to 8 cm*
*Flowering July to September*  *Annual*

## *Red-hot Pokers*

There are both small and tall varieties of this easily recognised plant. Each 'poker' is made up of many small flowers, which change from scarlet on the top to yellow lower down. The plant needs full sunlight and a well-drained soil.

*Height 30 cm to 2 metres*
*Flowering July to September*
*Flower size 7 to 30 cm*
*Perennial*

## Tobacco Plant

These are plants with a wide range of colours. Some species are strongly scented. The flowers will grow in sunny or partly-shaded flower beds.
The seeds should be sown under glass in March and planted out when the frosts have gone.

*Height 60 to 90 cm*
*Flowering July to September*
*Flower size 7 to 13 cm*
*Annual*

## Roses of Sharon

Another plant which will grow in dry shaded corners of the garden. When not in flower, the evergreen leaves form a dense mass and cover the ground.

*Height 50 to 80 cm*        *Flower size 5 to 7 cm*
*Flowering July to September*        *Perennial*

### French Marigolds

A much smaller plant than the African Marigold. There are many varieties, with a wide range of colours from dark red to bright yellow.

*Height 15 to 30 cm*
*Flowering July to October*
*Flower size 2 to 5 cm*
*Annual*

### Hydrangeas

A shrub with large flower heads. It is a popular indoor plant, but it grows well in gardens, especially near the seaside.

*Height 45 cm to 1.5 metres*
*Flowering July to October*
*Flower size 1 to 2 cm*
*Perennial shrub*

## *Montbretia*

A plant which needs a sunny position and a well-drained soil. In a heavy soil the bulbs often die through being too wet.

*Height 30 cm to 1 metre*
*Flowering July to October*
*Flower size 2 to 4 cm*
*Perennial bulb*

## *Golden Rod*

Golden rod will grow in almost any part of the garden and is often placed in corners where little else will grow.

*Height 50 cm to 2 metres*
*Flowering July to October*
*Flower size 1 to 2 mm*
*Perennial*

47

### Sunflowers

This giant of the garden is easily grown in well-drained soil. As its name would suggest, it needs sunshine. It grows from seed sown in April.

*Height 2 to 3 metres*
*Flowering July to October*
*Flower size 15 to 50 cm*
*Annual*

## August~September onwards

### Chrysanthemums

Many varieties of chrysanthemum exist and all of them make excellent cut flowers. Hardy border chrysanthemums are planted in ordinary soil during early spring in sunny positions.
Very large plants are grown in pots, which are taken into the greenhouse before the end of September — only one bud is allowed to develop. These plants are grown from cuttings taken each spring.

*Height 45 cm to 1.5 metres*
*Flowering August to October*
*Flower size 5 to 30 cm*

## Freesias

Freesias have a delicious fragrance. They are mainly a greenhouse plant but in warm places they can be grown in a sunny sheltered position.

*Height 30 to 45 cm*
*Flowering August to September,*
*winter and spring*
*under glass.*
*Flower size 3 to 5 cm*
*Half-hardy bulb*

## Dahlias

In good soil dahlias are easy to grow. There are many varieties, and they are grown from seeds or tubers. They need plenty of water and warm weather.
After the first frost, the plants die and the tubers must be dug up, cleaned and stored for the winter in a frost free place.

*Height 30 cm to 1.2 metres*
*Flowering August to October*
*Flower size 5 to 30 cm*
*Perennial*

49

### *Scabious*

Both annual and perennial varieties of scabious are to be found in gardens. They will grow in all good soils, but they do best in a sheltered position in full sunlight. They are excellent for cutting.
The flowers may be also red, pink or blue.

*Height 60 cm to 2 metres*
*Flowering August to October*
*Flower size 5 to 10 cm*
*Annual and perennial*

### *Nasturtiums*

A climbing plant which needs a sunny position and a poor soil or there will be more leaves than flowers! Seeds should be sown in March, where they are to flower.

*Height 1 to 2 metres*
*Flowering August to October*
*Flower size 3 to 5 cm*
*Annual*

## *Michaelmas Daisies*

Looking their best when many plants are grouped
together, the starlike flowers of the michaelmas daisy are
seen in late summer when many other garden flowers
have faded. Every two years the roots should be lifted
and divided.

*Height 10 cm to 3 metres*
*Flowering September to October*
*Flower size 3 to 7 cm*
*Perennial*

51

# INDEX